Understanding My Emotions

When I'm Worried

Understanding My Emotions

When I'm Angry
When I'm Embarrassed
When I'm Happy
When I'm Lonely
When I'm Overwhelmed
When I'm Sad
When I'm Scared
When I'm Sorry
When I'm Surprised
When I'm Worried

Understanding My Emotions

When I'm Worried

ALEXANDRA DALTON

**Understanding My Emotions
When I'm Worried**

Copyright © 2016 by Village Earth Press, a division of Harding House Publishing. All rights reserved. No part of this publication may be reproduced or transmitted in any form or by any means, electronic or mechanical, including photocopying, recording, taping, or any information storage and retrieval system, without permission from the publisher.

Village Earth Press
Vestal, New York 13850
www.villageearthpress.com

First Printing
9 8 7 6 5 4 3 2 1

Series ISBN (paperback): 978-1-62524-440-6
ISBN (paperback): 978-1-62524-385-0
ebook ISBN: 978-1-62524-141-2
    Library of Congress Control Number: 2014941251

Author: Dalton, Alexandra.

Contents

To the Teacher or Parent 7

When I'm Worried 8

Find Out More 42

Feeling Words 44

Index 46

Picture Credits 47

About the Author 48

To the Teacher or Parent

More than a hundred years ago, John Dewey insisted that the true purpose of schooling was not simply to teach children a trade but to train them in deeper habits of mind. Social-emotional learning builds on Dewey's theory further, suggesting that emotional skills are crucial to both academic performance and future success in life.

The research is definitive: emotional training is good for children! A recent study, reported in the *New York Times*, found that preschoolers who had even a single year of social-emotional training continued to perform better two years after they left the program; they were less aggressive and less anxious than children who hadn't participated in the program. Another study found that K-12 students who received some form of emotional instruction scored an average of 11 percentile points higher on standardized achievement tests. A similar study found a nearly 20 percent decrease in students' violent behaviors.

The goal of this series of books, UNDERSTANDING MY EMOTIONS, is to instill in young children a foundation of emotional intelligence. Use these books to help children learn to understand, identify, and regulate their emotions. Give them important tools that will serve them well for the rest of their lives!

When I'm Worried

I have feelings going on inside me all the time. Some of these feelings are in my arms or legs, in my stomach or my head. Those feelings can be good or bad. Some of them are itchy, like when I have a mosquito bite. Others hurt, like when I have a stomachache.

But I have a different kind of feeling going on inside me too. These feelings are called emotions. Happiness is an emotion, and so is anger and sadness. I feel many other emotions too. Some of them feel good, and some don't. They don't hurt like a stomachache, but they still feel bad.

One of the feelings I have sometimes is worry. Worry is one of the bad feelings. I feel worried when I think something sad or scary might happen tomorrow or next year. Nothing bad is happening right now—but I'm scared it WILL happen.

Another word for "worried" is ANXIOUS. It's a feeling that makes me feel sad and scared inside, but it's a quiet feeling. It doesn't usually make me cry or shout. When I worry, I just think and think about the bad thing that might happen. I can't seem to think about anything else. Even when I'm doing something else, like reading a book, I'm still feeling worried.

All emotions happen inside our heads. Some of them are connected to what's going on around us.

We feel angry when someone takes away something that's ours.

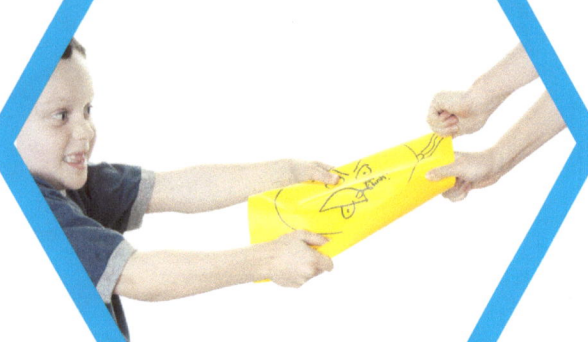

We feel happy when the sun shines.

We feel sad when we lose something we love.

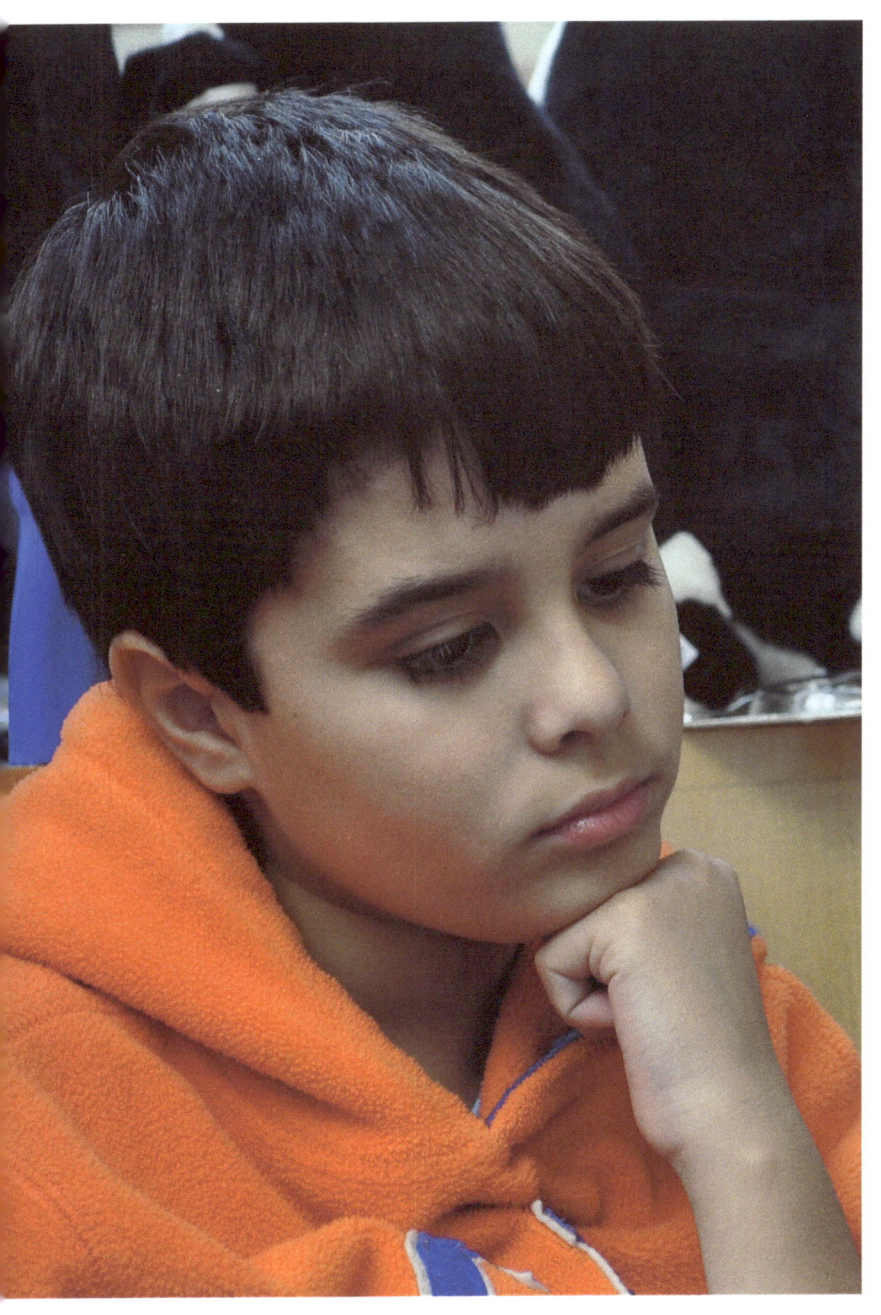

Feeling worried is a little different. It's not really connected to anything that's going on around us. It's connected to something we think MIGHT happen. Sometimes, the more we sit and think inside our own heads, the more worried we feel.

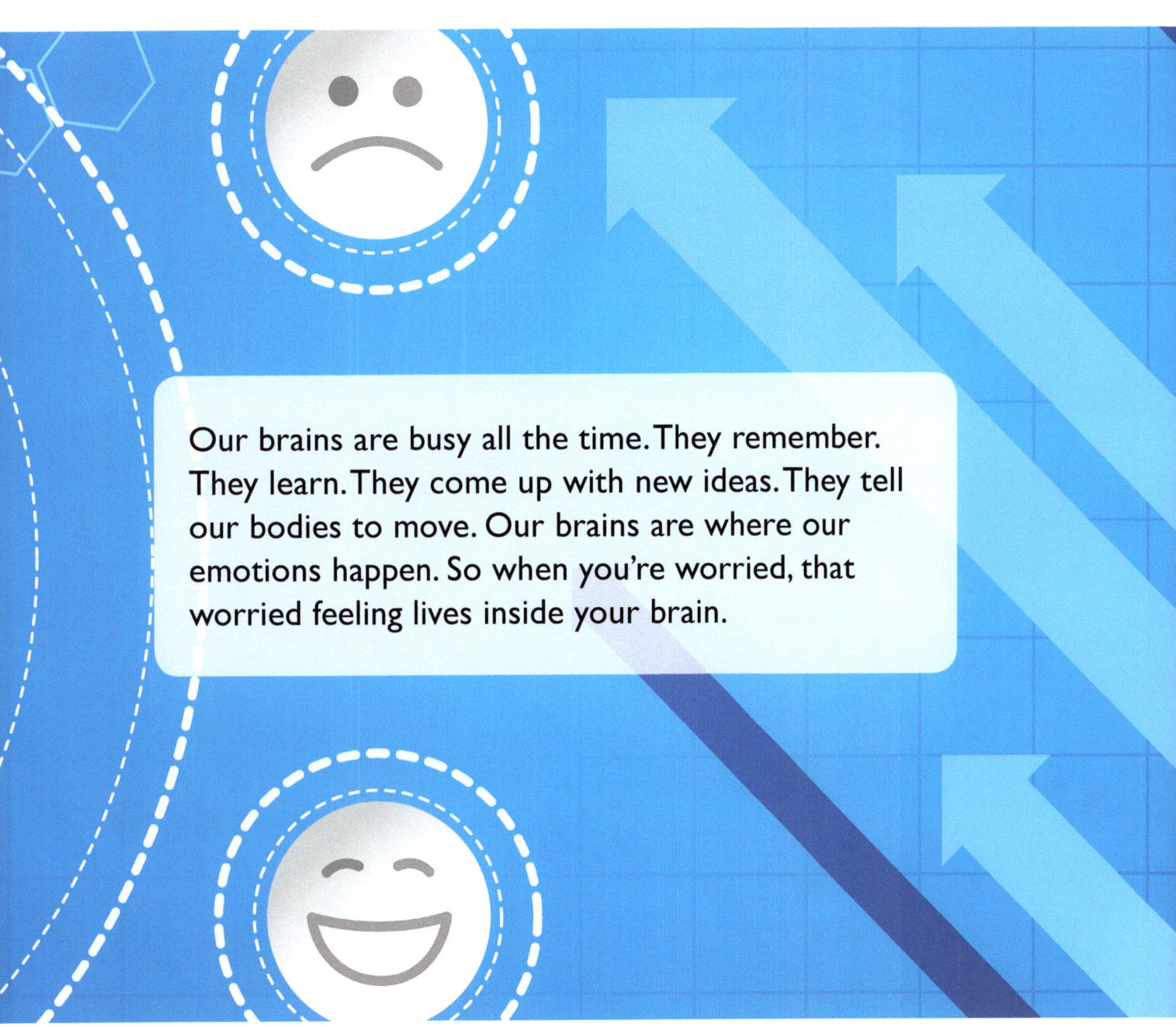

Our brains are busy all the time. They remember. They learn. They come up with new ideas. They tell our bodies to move. Our brains are where our emotions happen. So when you're worried, that worried feeling lives inside your brain.

Worry is a little like fear. It's not usually quite as strong, though. That's because whatever I'm worried about isn't usually in the room with me.

It could be far away—but I'm scared it's coming my way. One day I saw a scary dog in the park—and now whenever I go outside, I worry that the dog might have run all the way across town to my house!

Or it could be something that hasn't happened, but I think it could happen—like I worry that my mother might get really sick. She's not sick now—but what if she GOT sick?

My brother worries about things he imagines, that aren't even real—like scary monsters in the dark!

Even though worry starts out in my brain, it can make my whole body feel different. When I worry too much, it can make my stomach hurt.

It can give me a headache—and then it's hard for me to concentrate when I try to do my homework.

When I'm worried about something, it can make me have other emotions too. I might get mad easier. I yell at my brothers. I get cross with my parents. Sometimes I feel angry and I don't even know why.

Worry can make me sad too. When I feel worried, I feel like there's nothing right in the world!

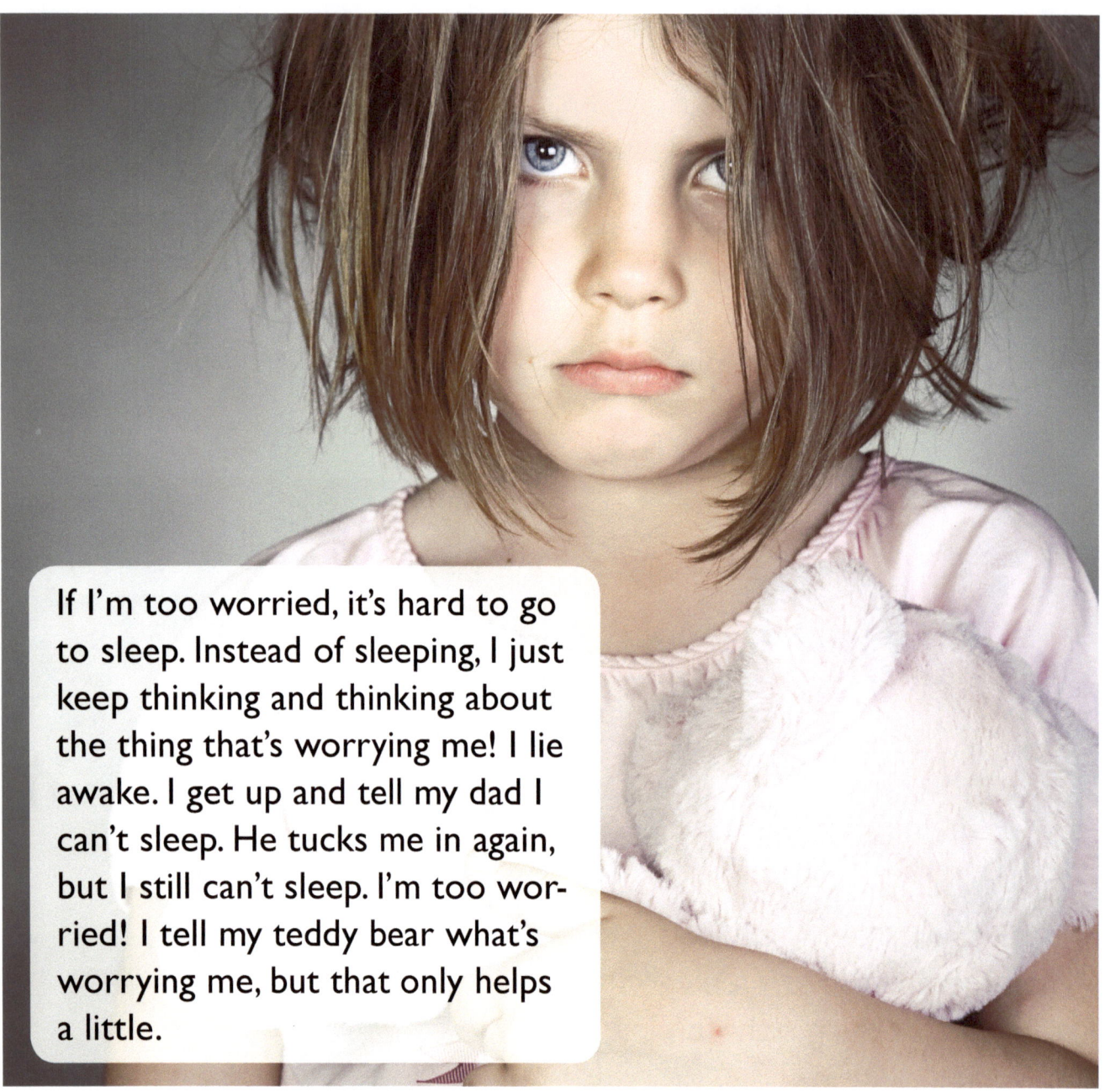

If I'm too worried, it's hard to go to sleep. Instead of sleeping, I just keep thinking and thinking about the thing that's worrying me! I lie awake. I get up and tell my dad I can't sleep. He tucks me in again, but I still can't sleep. I'm too worried! I tell my teddy bear what's worrying me, but that only helps a little.

When I worry like that, I need to tell a real person. If I just keep it inside, my worries can grow and grow—and make me feel more and more sad and scared.

I need to tell my parents. Sometimes I call my grandma on the phone, and I tell her. She's good at helping me handle my worries!

Lots of times, people can tell what I'm feeling just by looking at my face. My face tells people what I'm feeling inside.

They can tell when I'm happy by my smile.

My face tells them when I'm sad too. I hold my mouth differently when I'm sad. My eyes look sad.

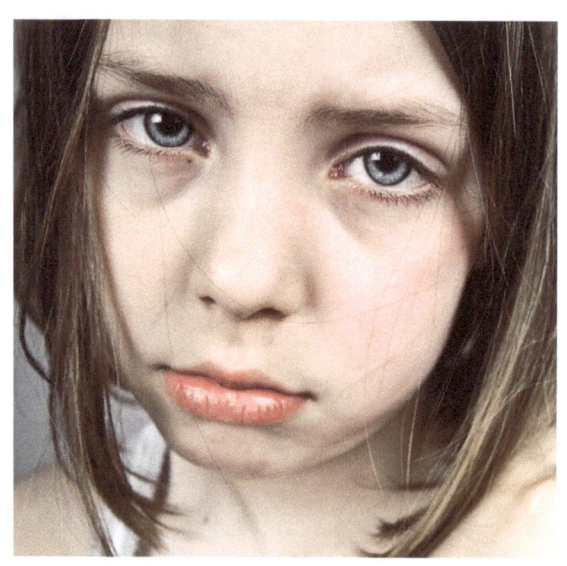

The way my face changes with my feeling is called my EXPRESSION. But people can't always tell I'm worried just by looking at my expression. They might just notice that I'm quieter than usual. Or they might think I have an upset face—but they don't know why. That's why I need to TELL someone when I'm worried!

Sometimes I can tell what other people are feeling by paying attention to their faces. The shape of their eyes and their mouths tell me what they're feeling. Even if they don't talk to me about their emotions, their expressions give me clues about what they're feeling inside.

I can tell when they're feeling happy.

I can tell when they're scared.

I can see when something has made them mad.

But I can't always tell when they're worried!

Grownups have the same emotions kids do. My dad says that sometimes he feels like laughing—and sometimes he feels like shouting because he's so angry.

He gets scared sometimes. He feels surprised and silly and bored. He feels all the things that I do!

And grownups get worried too. They just worry about different things than kids do.

My grandpa says he worries about his kids, even though they're all grown up.

My mom worries about money. She worries whether she and my dad will have enough money to pay for everything our family needs.

But my mom says I never need to worry about that. She says that grownup worries are for grownups to take care of.

I guess everyone has their own things they worry about.

My friend Jason says he worries every time his parents fight. He worries they will get a divorce, and he won't be able to live with both of them anymore. His parents explain to him that everyone gets angry sometimes but that doesn't mean they don't still love each other.

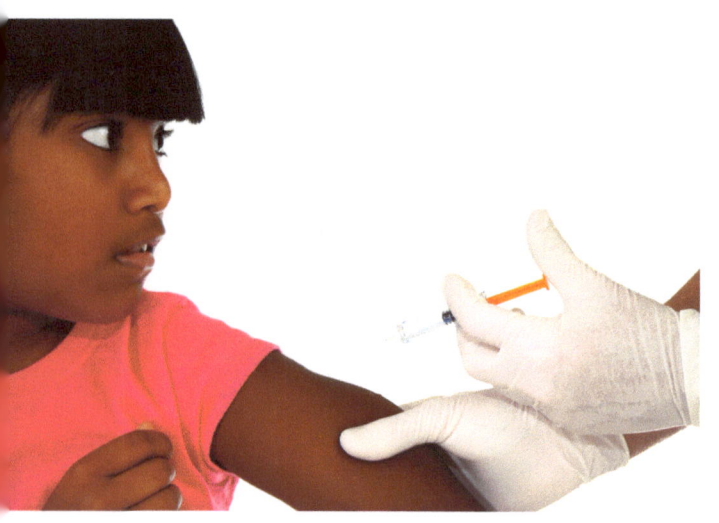

Anika worries about going to the doctor and getting a shot. The doctor tells her that she only needs a shot sometimes, not every time she goes to the doctor. Most times, she won't need any shots, but if she does, it only hurts for a second.

My friend Katie worries about tests. She worries that she won't get a good grade. Her mom tells her to study and then just do her best.

Every time there's a storm, my friend Malik worries that lightning will strike his house. His dad tells him that lightning doesn't hit houses very often, and even if it did, it probably wouldn't hurt the people inside the house.

Rebecca worries that a scary stranger will hurt her. Her mom tells her that most strangers are nice people, but Rebecca can take care of herself by learning how to stay safe.

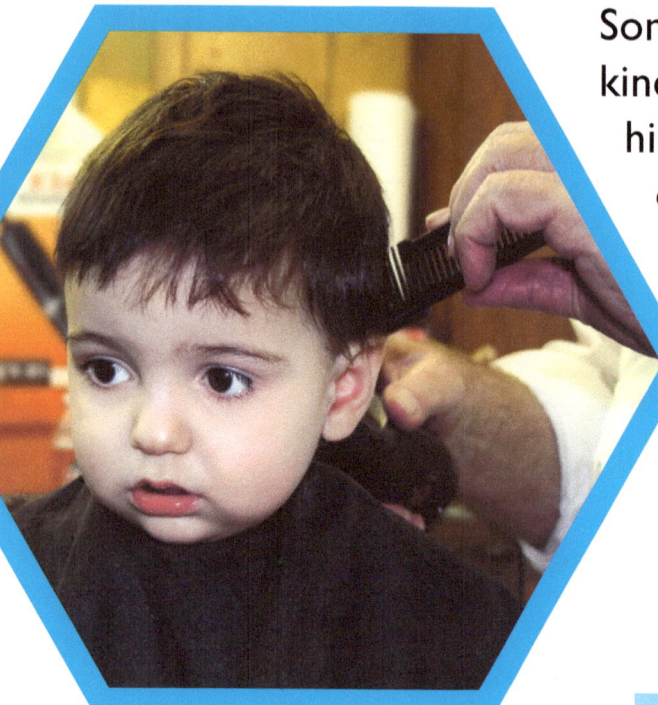

Sometimes other people's worries seem kind of silly. When my baby brother gets his hair cut, he worries the man will cut off his ear by mistake. That's silly! But my brother doesn't know that.

He worries about balloons too! He worries that they're going to pop.

When we tell my brother he doesn't need to worry about those things, it doesn't make his worry go away. He's still worried! His worries don't seem silly to him.

 When I look back at all the things that I used to worry about when I was younger, some of them seem pretty silly too! I used to worry that monsters were hiding in my closet at night.

And I worried that an alien would land in our backyard.

These worries didn't seem silly when I was younger. Now that I've learned more, though, I know that monsters and aliens aren't real.

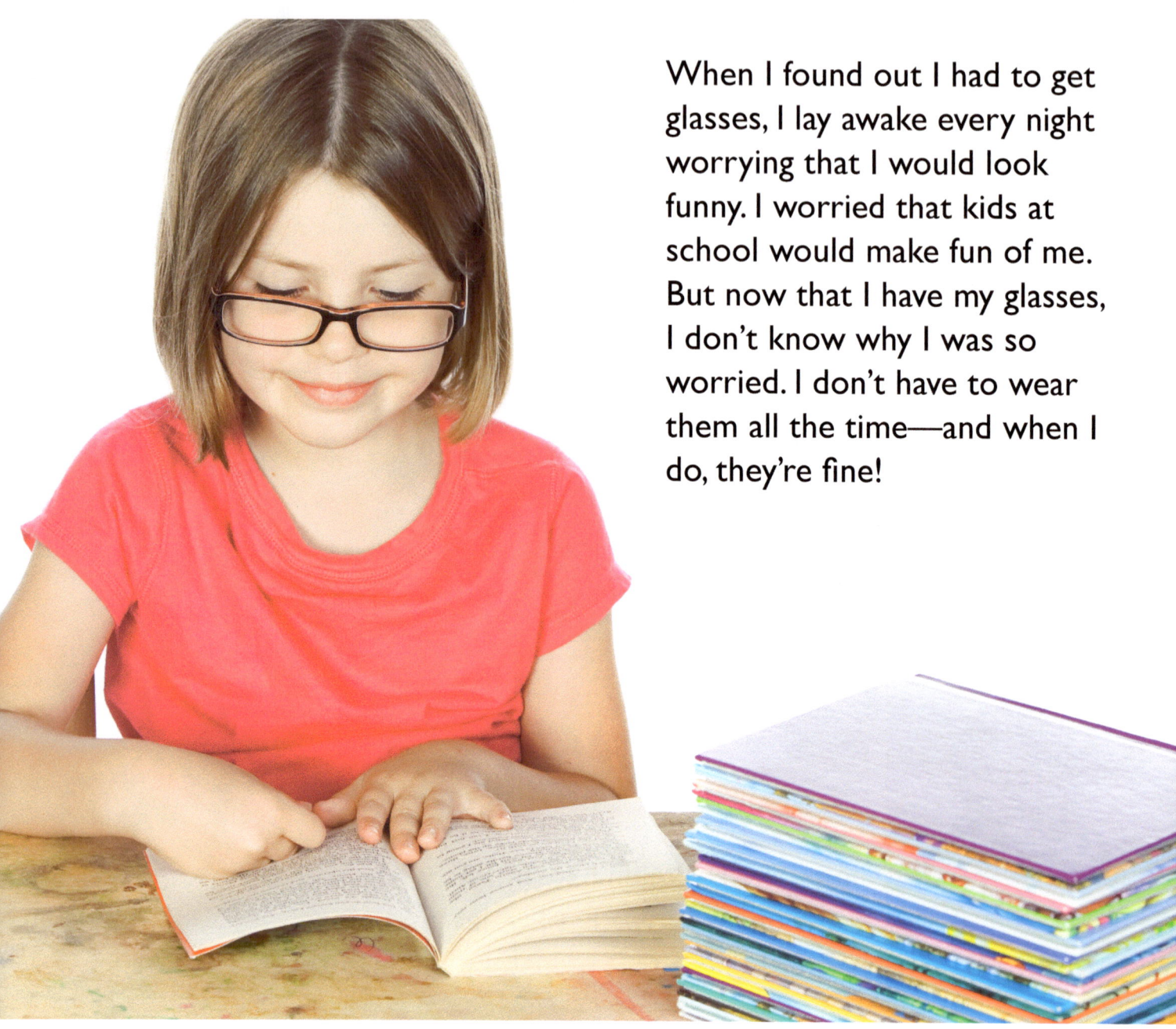

When I found out I had to get glasses, I lay awake every night worrying that I would look funny. I worried that kids at school would make fun of me. But now that I have my glasses, I don't know why I was so worried. I don't have to wear them all the time—and when I do, they're fine!

My mom says that's the way worries turn out a lot of the time. Most of the things we worry about don't ever happen—or they turn out not to be so bad if they do happen. Like when I finally met that black dog I'd worried about so much. In my imagination, he looked like a big scary wolf. But it turned out he was just a friendly dog.

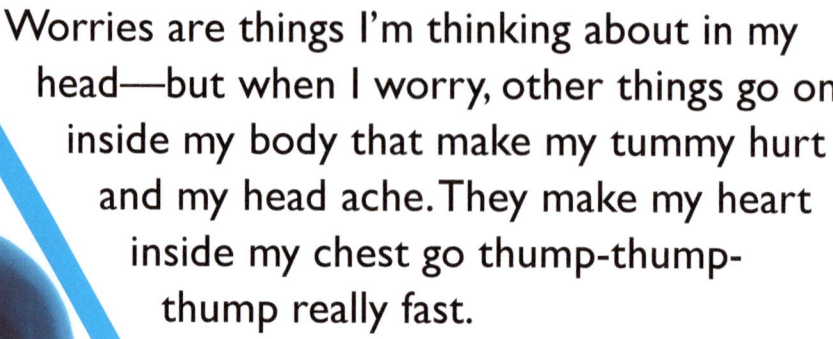

Worries are things I'm thinking about in my head—but when I worry, other things go on inside my body that make my tummy hurt and my head ache. They make my heart inside my chest go thump-thump-thump really fast.

A long, long time ago, people had to deal with lots of dangers—like wild animals chasing them. People's bodies learned to do one of two things: run away or fight. Their bodies got them ready to do one or the other.

My mom says all those feelings inside my body—my tummy ache, my headache, and my pounding heart—were meant to get me ready to face danger. But now they are kind of like smoke alarms that go off when there's no fire! Things SEEM dangerous, and my body is getting ready to run away or fight. But I can't really run away and there's nothing to fight. So all those feelings turn into worry.

Now that I understand all that, I like to think of worry as a kind of monster. I don't have to let the Worry Monster boss me around. I can tell him to go away!

Going outside and riding my bike chases away the Worry Monster.

There are different things I can do to make the Worry Monster go away. I can practice thinking happy thoughts at bedtime.

Doing something fun with my mom makes the Worry Monster go away too.

Acting goofy and silly helps too. Good feelings get rid of the Worry Monster!

Now when I get that funny feeling in my tummy and I feel my heart start to beat fast, I know the Worry Monster is somewhere near. When I start to think the same scary things over and over, I know that's the Worry Monster. When I start thinking that something bad MIGHT happen, it's just that same old silly monster. I take deep breaths and think happy thoughts. I find something fun to do. I kiss that old Worry Monster good-bye!

Everybody feels worried sometimes. The Worry Monster comes to see everyone once in a while.

The next time YOU'RE worried, here's what you can do:

- First, you need to know that the Worry Monster is trying to get you. Are you thinking about something scary or sad that MIGHT happen? Does your tummy feel funny? Is your heart pounding? All those are signs that the Worry Monster is nearby. Once you know he's there, you can tell him to go away!

- Try to learn more about what worries you. Usually, the more you know and understand, the less worried you'll feel. So go to the library and read books about what worries you. Look online. Ask your parents and teachers questions. You may discover that the thing you thought MIGHT happen, probably won't—or that if it does happen, it won't be as bad as you thought.

- Talk to someone you trust. When the grownups in your life know you're worried, they can help you.

- Take deep breaths and try to relax. Do something fun that will make you think about other things.

- Find something to smile about. Think happy thoughts.

- Let the Worry Monster know that you don't need him to hang around. There's nothing you need to run away from. There's nothing to fight.

Tell the Worry Monster to get lost!

Find Out More

You can learn more about your emotions by going online and checking out these websites. Some of the sites have videos you can watch or games you can play. You could also read the other books in this series to find out more about feelings—or you could go to your library and see if you can find the books listed on the next page. There's a lot more you can learn about feelings!

On the Internet

It's My Life: Emotions
pbskids.org/itsmylife/emotions

KidsHealth: Feelings
kidshealth.org/kid/feeling

Model Me: Faces and Emotions
www.modelmekids.com/emotions_dvd.html

In Books

Adams, Christine A. *Worry, Worry, Go Away!: A Kid's Book About Worry and Anxiety.* St. Meinrad, IN: Abbey Press, 2012.

Cook, Julia. *Wilma Jean the Worry Machine.* Chattanooga, TN: National Center for Youth Issues, 2012.

Crist, James. *What to Do When You're Scared and Worried: A Guide for Kids.* Minneapolis, MN: Free Spirit Publishing, 2004.

Guanci, Anne Marie. *David and the Worry Beast.* Far Hills, NJ: New Horizon Press, 2010.

Helsley, Donalisa. *The Worry Glasses: Overcoming Anxiety.* Milwaukee, WI: Mirror Publishing, 2012.

Huebner, Dawn. *Sometimes I Worry Too Much, But Now I Know How to Stop.* New York: Virtual Help, 2003.

Huebner, Dawn. *What to Do When You Worry Too Much.* Washington, DC: Magination Press, 2005.

Feeling Words

Happy and sad are two of the words we use when we talk about feelings. But there are many more words that describe feelings. Here are some of those words.

Excited

Angry

Embarrassed

Lonely

Guilty

Hurt

Proud

Scared

Shy

Sorry

Surprised

Bored

Index

An index is a way you can quickly find something inside a book. The numbers tell you exactly what page to go to if you want to find that word.

angry (anger) 9, 12, 19, 24, 28, 44
anxious 11

bedtime 37
bodies 15, 18, 34–35
book 11, 40, 42–43
bored 25, 45
brain 14–15, 18
brother 17, 19, 30

dad 20, 24, 27, 29
danger 34–35
dog 16, 33

expression 22–23
eyes 22–23

face 22–23, 35, 42
fear 16
friend 28–29
fun 32, 38–39, 41

glasses 32, 43

grandma 21
grandpa 26
grownups 24, 26–27, 40

happy (happiness) 9, 12, 22–23, 37, 39, 41, 44
head 9, 12–14, 34–35
headache 18
heart 34–35, 39–40
homework 18

imagination 33

library 40, 42
lightning 29

mad 19, 23
money 27
monster 17, 31, 36–41
mother (mom) 17, 27, 29, 33, 35, 38
mouth 22–23

online 40, 42

parents 19, 21, 28, 40

reading 11

sad (sadness) 9–12, 19, 21–22, 40, 44
school 32
sick 17
silly 25, 30–31, 38–39
sleep 20
smile 22, 41
stomachache (tummy ache) 35
stranger 29
surprised 25, 45

teacher 40
teddy bear 20
test 29
thoughts 37, 39–41

website 42
Worry Monster 36–41

Picture Credits

p. 8: © Eladora | Dreamstime.com
p. 9: © Jmpaget | Dreamstime.com
p. 10: © Jmpaget | Dreamstime.com
p. 11: © Jmpaget | Dreamstime.com
p. 12: © Dbirdinparadise | Dreamstime.com, © Cheryl Casey | Dreamstime.com, © Constantin Opris | Dreamstime.com
p. 13: © Canettistock | Dreamstime.com
p. 14–15: © Artisticco Llc | Dreamstime.com
p. 16: © Jmpaget | Dreamstime.com, © Kirsten Broadbent | Dreamstime.com
p. 17: © Photographerlondon | Dreamstime.com, © Khakimullin Aleksandr | Dreamstime.com
p. 18: © Maxximmm | Dreamstime.com, © Jmpaget | Dreamstime.com
p. 19: © Jmpaget | Dreamstime.com
p. 20: © Jmpaget | Dreamstime.com
p. 21: © Jmpaget | Dreamstime.com
p. 22: © Jmpaget | Dreamstime.com
p. 23: © Spotmatik | Dreamstime.com, © Kati1313 | Dreamstime.com, © Jesse Kunerth | Dreamstime.com, © Liquidphoto | Dreamstime.com
p. 24: © Tomnex | Dreamstime.com
p. 25: © Tomnex | Dreamstime.com
p. 26: © Andrew Bassett | Dreamstime.com
p. 27: © Christine Langer-püschel | Dreamstime.com
p. 28 © Wavebreakmedia Ltd | Dreamstime.com, © Photoeuphoria | Dreamstime.com
p. 29: © Tatyana Chernyak | Dreamstime.com, © Nathan Allred | Dreamstime.com, © Madartists | Dreamstime.com
p. 30: © Photoeuphoria | Dreamstime.com
p. 31: © Gizwiz | Dreamstime.com, © Alexmax | Dreamstime.com
p. 32: © Jmpaget | Dreamstime.com
p. 33: © Jmpaget | Dreamstime.com
p. 34: © Ancroft | Dreamstime.com, © Cory Thoman | Dreamstime.com
p. 35: © Leerodney Avison | Dreamstime.com
p. 36: © Jmpaget | Dreamstime.com, © Renomartin | Dreamstime.com
p. 37: © Jmpaget | Dreamstime.com
p. 38: © Jmpaget | Dreamstime.com
p. 39: © Jmpaget | Dreamstime.com
p. 40: © Jmpaget | Dreamstime.com, © Renomartin | Dreamstime.com
p. 41: © Jmpaget | Dreamstime.com
p. 44: Fotolia: © Fasphotographic, © Cantor Pannato, © Andres Rodriguez, © Gabriel Blaj, © Moodboard Premium, © Halfpoint
p. 45: Fotolia: © Cantor Pannato, © Blend Images, © Zhekos, © Olly, © Wavebreak Media Micro; © Serrnovik | Dreamstime.com

About the Author

Alexandra Dalton was a teacher, and now she is a writer. When she was a teacher, she helped her students talk about their feelings. She knows that it's hard work sometimes to talk about our feelings—but she knows we feel better and we get along with each other better when we can use our words to talk about how we feel. Alexandra has three children. She also has a dog and a cat and four goats. She lives in New York State.

www.ingramcontent.com/pod-product-compliance
Lightning Source LLC
Chambersburg PA
CBHW061359090426
42743CB00002B/74